PRESENTS

The Wonderful World of Knowledge

MAMMALS

Using The Wonderful World of Knowledge

Mickey, Minnie, Donald, Daisy, Goofy, and Pluto are ready to take you on an adventure ride through the world of learning. Discover the secrets of science, nature, our world, the past, and much more. Climb aboard and enjoy the ride.

Look here for a general summary of the theme

Labels tell *you what's happening in the pictures*

Mickey's ears *lead you to one of the main topics*

The pictures by *themselves can tell you a lot, even before you read a word*

Watch out for special pages where Mickey takes a close look at some key ideas

The Solar System

The Solar System is the name given to our Sun and its family of planets. It also includes the moons, millions of pieces of rock called asteroids and meteors, and frozen lumps of dust and ice called comets. Everything else you can see in the sky is outside the Solar System and is far, far away. Every single star is itself a sun, and each may have its own family of planets and moons.

Saturn is surrounded by beautiful rings

REPTILES AND AMPHIBIANS

Color and Camouflage

Frogs and toads come in nearly every imaginable color, even gold or black. They have a wide range of patterns, from spots and stripes to zigzags.

Color and pattern help frogs and toads survive. Bright colors warn that they may be poisonous. Drab colors camouflage them, or hide them against their background. Many tree frogs are exactly the same green as leaves, while others look like bark. The Asian horned toad has the best camouflage of all. Folds of patchy, brown skin and a flat body make it look like a dead leaf when it lies still on the forest floor.

Folds of brown skin give perfect camouflage

Flat body is hard to see among dead leaves

Asian horned toad

False-eyed frog

Markings look like eyes

For extra protection, bad-smelling liquid oozes out around false eyes

FALSE-EYED FROG
The South American false-eyed frog has large markings on its flanks that look like eyes. These fool some predators into thinking that they are looking at a much larger animal, such as a cat or bird.

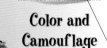

Dog sniffing curiously at the toad

COLOR AND CAMOUFLAGE

Strawberry arrow frog

POISON-DART FROGS
Deadly poison oozes from the skin of Central and South American poison-dart frogs. People in the rain forest rub the tips of their arrows and blowpipe darts on the skin of these frogs to collect the poison to use for hunting.

Blue poison-dart frog

Oriental fire-bellied toad defending itself against a dog

Skin oozes a stinging fluid

Bright colored belly

Green and black back

FIRE-BELLIED TOAD
When cornered by a predator, the Oriental fire-bellied toad of eastern Asia arches its back and rears up on its legs to show its fiery underside. Wise attackers back off, because the toad's skin oozes a stinging, bad-tasting fluid.

Toad rears up on its back legs

FIND OUT MORE
MAMMALS: Camouflage
PLANET EARTH: Forests

16   17

Mickey's page *numbers help you look things up. Don't forget there's a glossary and index at the back of each book*

Goofy and his *friends know how to give you a chuckle on every topic*

Mickey points you to more information in other books in your *The Wonderful World of Knowledge*

FIND OUT MORE
MAMMALS: Camouflage
PLANET EARTH: Forests

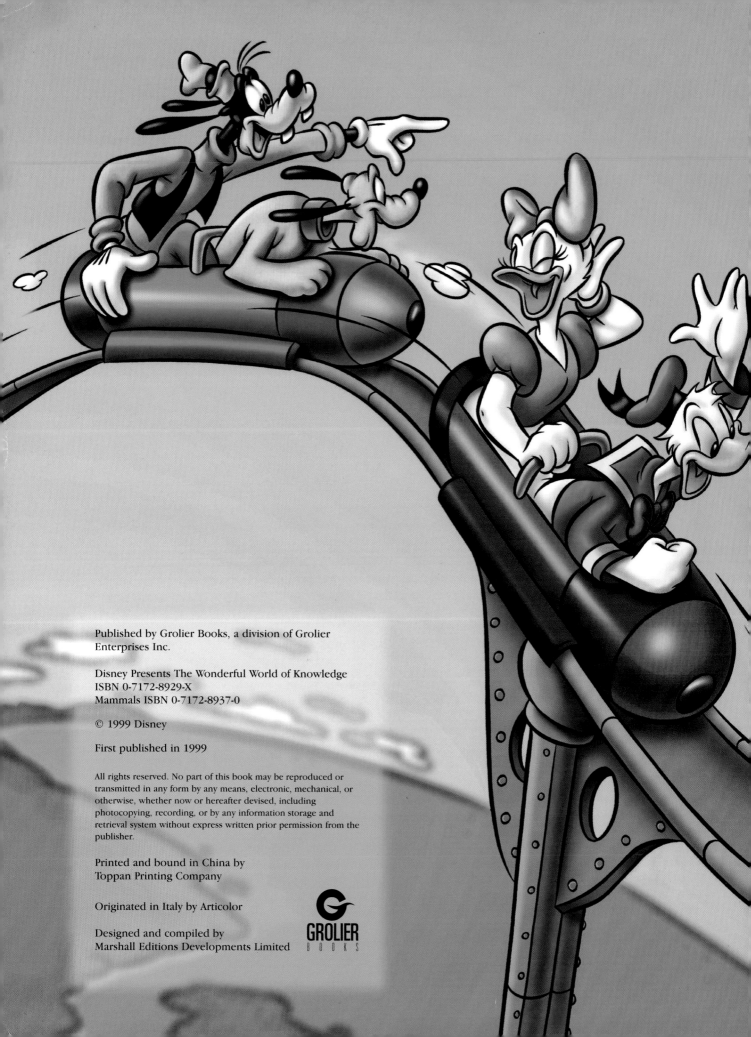

Published by Grolier Books, a division of Grolier
Enterprises Inc.

Disney Presents The Wonderful World of Knowledge
ISBN 0-7172-8929-X
Mammals ISBN 0-7172-8937-0

© 1999 Disney

First published in 1999

Printed and bound in China by
Toppan Printing Company

Originated in Italy by Articolor

Designed and compiled by
Marshall Editions Developments Limited

GROLIER
BOOKS

Your favorite characters present some facts to astound you and your friends

THE SOLAR SYSTEM

HOW OUR SOLAR SYSTEM WAS FORMED

1 The Solar System formed 4.6 billion years ago. It started at the center of an enormous swirling cloud of gas and dust.

2 The Sun burst into flames and became a star. Its light and warmth spread throughout the new Solar System.

3 Gas and dust left over from making the Sun clumped together in places. These clumps grew bigger and formed the planets.

4 The planets closest to the Sun are small and made from rock and metal. The larger outer planets are made from gas and liquid.

AMAZING FACTS

★ The Sun is enormous compared to the planets. It is nearly 1,000 times more massive than the giant planet Jupiter.

Numbers lead *you step-by-step through how things happen*

Colorful boxes *zoom in on information*

Pluto is the farthest planet from the Sun

Each planet has its own path, or orbit

Planet orbits

ORBITING THE SUN
No matter how still you try to be, you are always moving. This is because the Earth – and all the other planets – are moving. They are flying through Space around the Sun in looping paths called orbits.

Neptune is a cold, blue planet

Uranus is tipped over on its side

THE "PULL" OF GRAVITY
If you throw a ball into the air, it comes down again. The invisible force that pulls it down to Earth is called gravity. The Earth's gravity holds us down on the ground. The Sun's gravity is strong enough to hold all its planets in their orbits.

Gravity pulls a ball to Earth

rs is red *dusty*   The Solar System

FIND OUT MORE
PLANET EARTH: Night and day
SCIENCE ALL AROUND US: Gravity

Mickey's helpers test some ideas themselves

Contents

Mammals

The fiercest tiger and the friendliest kitten, the biggest elephant and the smallest mouse – they are all mammals. There are thousands of different kinds of mammals, living all kinds of fascinating lives on and under the land, in the sea, and in the air.

When we think of mammals, our feelings vary from fearful respect for the lordly lion to delighted love for our pets. We depend on mammals for food and as workers in our fields and farms. We humans are mammals ourselves.

What is a Mammal?

If you want to see a mammal, look in a mirror. Humans are one of about 4,000 kinds of animals called mammals. All mammals are warm blooded – they can keep an even temperature inside their bodies. They have lungs for breathing air and a bony frame called a skeleton. Most mammals have large brains and good senses of smell, taste, touch, sight, and hearing. They also have at least some hair or fur on their skin.

Skull

Backbone

Ribcage

Flippers

Dolphin, a sea mammal

THE FIRST MAMMALS

The earliest mammals were small animals like shrews that fed on insects and dinosaur eggs. They lived about 200 million years ago.

Zalambdalestes,
an early mammal

MAMMAL SKELETON

All mammals have a backbone made of separate bones called vertebrae. Some parts of the skeleton have changed to suit the lives of different mammals. Sea mammals, for example, have flippers instead of legs.

COOLING DOWN

When they get hot, mammals can cool down by sweating. Sweat glands produce water, which dries on the surface of the skin. This process takes heat away from the body.

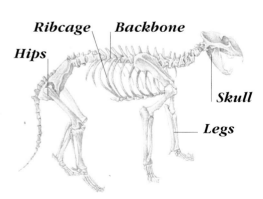

Ribcage   Backbone

Hips

Skull

Legs

Lion, a land mammal

Sweating child

AMAZING FACTS

★ **Largest of all mammals is the enormous blue whale. It weighs up to 190 tonnes, more than 30 African elephants.**

EGG-LAYING MAMMALS

Most mammals give birth to live young, but there are two types that lay eggs. They are the echidna and the platypus. Their young still drink mother's milk.

Australian echidna

FEEDING BABIES

A female mammal has special body parts called mammary glands, which produce milk for her babies. The baby sucks the milk from the glands through nipples, or teats.

Thick fur helps keep the body warm

Mammary gland on the mother's chest

***Baby orangutan** feeding through a nipple*

***Large hands** for holding onto branches*

Tree nest that the orangutan sleeps in at night

FIND OUT MORE
BIRDS: Eggs
HUMAN BODY: Skeleton

Female orangutan with baby

Pouched Mammals

☞Kangaroos, Tasmanian devils, koalas, opossums, and sugar gliders are all marsupials – a special type of mammal. The word marsupial means "pouched mammal." Most marsupials have a furry pouch like a pocket on the belly. Their young live in here for the first few months of their lives. There are more than 250 different kinds of marsupials. Most live in Australasia and South America.

AMAZING FACTS

★ A newborn red kangaroo is just 2 cm (¾ in) long – about the size of a thimble.

Baby kangaroo in the pouch

Adult kangaroos eat grass and other plants

Fur of female and young red kangaroos is grayish-brown

RED KANGAROO
Red kangaroos live in the outback of Australia. Females give birth to a single baby called a joey. The joey lives in its mother's pouch, feeding on her milk. Larger joeys leave the pouch, but they dive back for safety if danger threatens.

Tail props the kangaroo up as it stands on its back legs

Koala with baby

Baby koala travels on its mother's back when it leaves the pouch

Strong back legs for hopping along at high speed

Large feet have four toes

SLEEPY KOALA
The Australian koala sleeps for up to 18 hours a day. It spends the rest of its time climbing trees and feeding on eucalyptus leaves.

Long ears
*for picking up
every sound*

Long face allows
room for large teeth

Short front legs
*for leaning on
while feeding*

Pouch where
*young live and
feed in safety*

A joey feeds
*on its mother's
milk until it is
about a year old*

**Female red kangaroos
and their young**

Tail helps the
glider balance

The glider steers
*by changing the
position of its
skin flaps*

Sugar glider

GLIDING MARSUPIAL

To move from tree to tree, the sugar glider leaps into the air with its legs outstretched. This opens out flaps of skin at its sides. The flaps act like a parachute, so the glider can sail up to 50 m (165 ft) through the air.

Wooly opossum

FRUIT FEEDER

The wooly opossum usually lives in the tropical rain forest trees of Central and South America. It feeds on fruit and nectar, the sweet liquid in flowers.

BONE CRUSHER

The jaws of the Tasmanian devil are so strong that it can crush bones and eat every bit of another animal. This fierce marsupial lives on the Australian island of Tasmania. It hunts reptiles, birds, fish, and small mammals.

Tasmanian devil

FIND OUT MORE
ATLAS OF THE WORLD: Australia
PLANET EARTH: Marsupials

Insect-eaters

Some mammals, including moles, shrews, and hedgehogs, live by eating large numbers of insects. They also eat other small creatures, such as worms and spiders. Many of these mammals have long, narrow snouts to reach into the small spaces where insects hide. They have strong claws for digging and sharp teeth to crunch up their food. Most insect-eaters live in warm areas, where there are always lots of insects.

UNDERGROUND DIGGER

A mole spends most of its life digging in the ground in search of insects and worms to eat. It uses its broad front legs to push earth aside as it digs. The mole's eyesight is poor, but it has good hearing.

Sharp claws
for digging

Mole leaving its burrow

Earth mound

Underground tunnels

Entrance to burrow

Mole's underground burrow

Armadillo sniffing for food

ARMORED ARMADILLO

An armadillo's body is heavily armored with bony plates. It may look fierce, but the armadillo is actually a gentle creature, which rolls up into a ball when attacked. It spends most of the day sleeping in the safety of a burrow, a hole underground. It digs the burrow with the help of its strong claws.

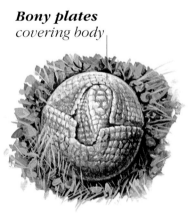

Bony plates
covering body

Armadillo rolled up in a ball

Moonrat in Borneo forest

NIGHT-TIME HUNTER

The moonrat stinks! It marks out
its territory, the area in which it lives,
with a rotten garlic smell made by
its scent glands. This Southeast Asian
mammal is about the size of a pet cat.
It usually hunts for its food at night.

AMAZING FACTS

★ The tiny Savi's white-
toothed shrew weighs
only 2 g ($^7/_{100}$ oz), less
than a teaspoon of
sugar. It is the smallest shrew and
one of the world's tiniest mammals.

Ridge of shaggy
bristles along
the back

**Giant anteater
feeding on ants**

Bushy tail
is almost as
long as the
body

INSECT FEAST

When a giant anteater finds an
ants' or termites' nest, it breaks
it open with its claws. It then
pushes its long nose inside and
laps up the insects with its
tongue. An anteater can eat as
many as 30,000 ants in a day.

Long nose for poking
into insects' nests

Tongue flicks
in and out up to
150 times a minute

Tongue is covered
with spines to help
trap the insects

Each front foot
has long claws for
digging into nests

FIND OUT MORE
INSECTS AND SPIDERS:
Ants, Termites

Amazon Rain Forest

In tropical rain forests, sometimes called jungles, it is always hot and there is plenty of rain. There are rain forests in Africa, Australia, Asia, and in Central and South America. The largest rain forest is in Brazil, around the Amazon River.

The huge Amazon rain forest is full of animal life. Mammals include monkeys, jaguars, tapirs, sloths, porcupines, anteaters, and opossums. Smaller mammals usually live in the trees, where there are plenty of leaves, flowers, and fruit to eat. Larger mammals stay on the forest floor. They hunt other animals or dig for plant roots or insects.

SWINGING FROM TREE TO TREE

1 **To get from one tree** to another, a spider monkey grips a branch with its tail and one hand.

2 **It then swings** itself forward and grasps another branch with both hands.

Camouflage shirt

Shady hat

A human explorer needs camouflaging clothes to help him hide so he can watch rain forest animals

Long trousers *for protection from stinging insects and plants*

BRAZILIAN TAPIR
The chunky tapir uses its long nose to sniff out tasty leaves on the forest floor. This shy mammal is a strong swimmer and spends much of its time in water.

Tapir looking for food

Long claws for *booking over branches*

Three-toed sloth and baby

Greenish fur *keeps the sloth hidden*

3 The monkey lets go of the first branch and curls its tail around the new branch.

Young sloths *cling tightly to their mothers*

TREE DWELLERS

Mammals that live mainly in the trees need to be able to cling on tightly. Many have strong hands and feet for hanging from branches. A long tail helps balance and can also be used for holding on.

Golden *mane*

Silky golden fur

The sloth hangs *upside-down from trees*

Tree porcupine

Golden lion tamarin

Sharp quills cover *the porcupine's body and protect it from enemies*

Long fingers *for handling food*

Sharp *claws*

The tamarin *lives in family groups in the trees*

FIND OUT MORE
ATLAS OF THE WORLD: Brazil
PLANET EARTH: Rain forest

Tail is almost *as long as the body*

Bats

Bats may be ugly or even scary to look at, but they are truly special. They are the only mammals that can fly. These furry-bodied creatures swoop through the air on smooth, hairless wings made of skin. Bats are found all over the world except in the Arctic and Antarctic. Most hunt at night. Many bats eat insects, but others feed on fruit, fish, frogs, mice, and other small animals.

Fruit bats suck the juice and soft pulp from fruit

FRUIT-EATING BATS

Fruit bats are sometimes called flying foxes, because of their foxlike faces. Fruit bats live in tropical places such as Southeast Asia and northern Australia. They eat ripe, juicy fruit and lap up nectar – a sweet liquid in flowers.

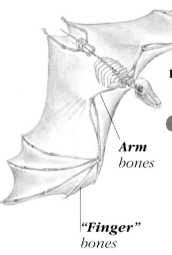

Wing

Bat skeleton

Arm bones

"Finger" bones

BONY SUPPORT

The extra-long bones of a bat's "hand" support the thin, rubbery skin of its wings. The bat's bones are very light so it can fly through the air.

FIERCE FACES

The strange lumps and folds on a bat's face affect the sounds it makes. Each type of bat has its own special calls that it makes when feeding or flying in the dark.

Leaf-nosed bat

Ghost-faced bat

Free-tailed bat

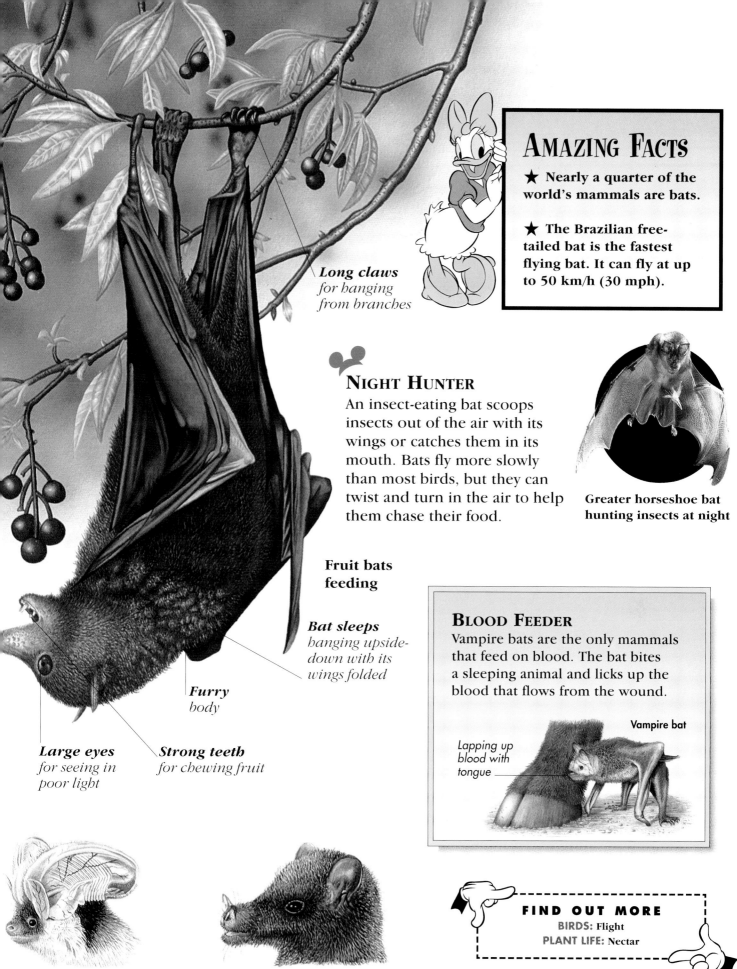

Long claws
*for hanging
from branches*

NIGHT HUNTER

An insect-eating bat scoops insects out of the air with its wings or catches them in its mouth. Bats fly more slowly than most birds, but they can twist and turn in the air to help them chase their food.

Greater horseshoe bat
hunting insects at night

**Fruit bats
feeding**

Bat sleeps
*hanging upside-
down with its
wings folded*

Furry
body

Large eyes
*for seeing in
poor light*

Strong teeth
for chewing fruit

BLOOD FEEDER

Vampire bats are the only mammals that feed on blood. The bat bites a sleeping animal and licks up the blood that flows from the wound.

Vampire bat

Lapping up
blood with
tongue

Spotted bat

Long-nosed bat

FIND OUT MORE
BIRDS: Flight
PLANT LIFE: Nectar

Monkeys and other Primates

Monkeys are close relatives of humans. People, monkeys, lemurs, tarsiers, and apes all belong to a group of about 200 different kinds of animals called primates. Primates are intelligent and quick to learn new skills. Many have long tails and live in trees. All primates have forward-pointing eyes, strong fingers for gripping, and long arms. Most have special thumbs that can move across their palms to press against the fingers. This means they can hold even small objects tightly.

Tarsier clinging to bamboo

NIGHT EYES
Each of the tarsier's huge eyes weighs more than its brain. The tarsier is active at night, when its enormous eyes help to make it a successful hunter of insects, birds, snakes, and lizards.

GROOMING FUR
Like all primates, baboons spend much of their day grooming themselves and each other. Grooming is an important social activity as well as a way of keeping the fur clean. Many other kinds of mammals also groom each other's fur.

The groomer picks out dirt and insects from the fur

Baboons grooming

LEAPING LEMUR

Early in the morning, lemurs climb up to the treetops in Madagascan forests to sun themselves after the cold night. With their long hind legs, they can leap from tree to tree in search of fruit and seeds.

Ring-tailed lemur in the middle of a jump

Bare face surrounded by fur

Long silky fur

The howler's voice echoes in a special area below the jaw

Powerful arms and legs

NOISY MONKEYS

The male red howler monkey of South America has one of the loudest voices of any animal. Sometimes a group of males from a troop of monkeys join together in a deafening chorus of howling that can be heard up to 3 km (2 miles) away. The sound warns other howler monkeys to stay away.

Red howler monkeys

Long tail for gripping branches

Strong fingers

FIND OUT MORE
HUMAN BODY: Hands
PLANT LIFE: Bamboo

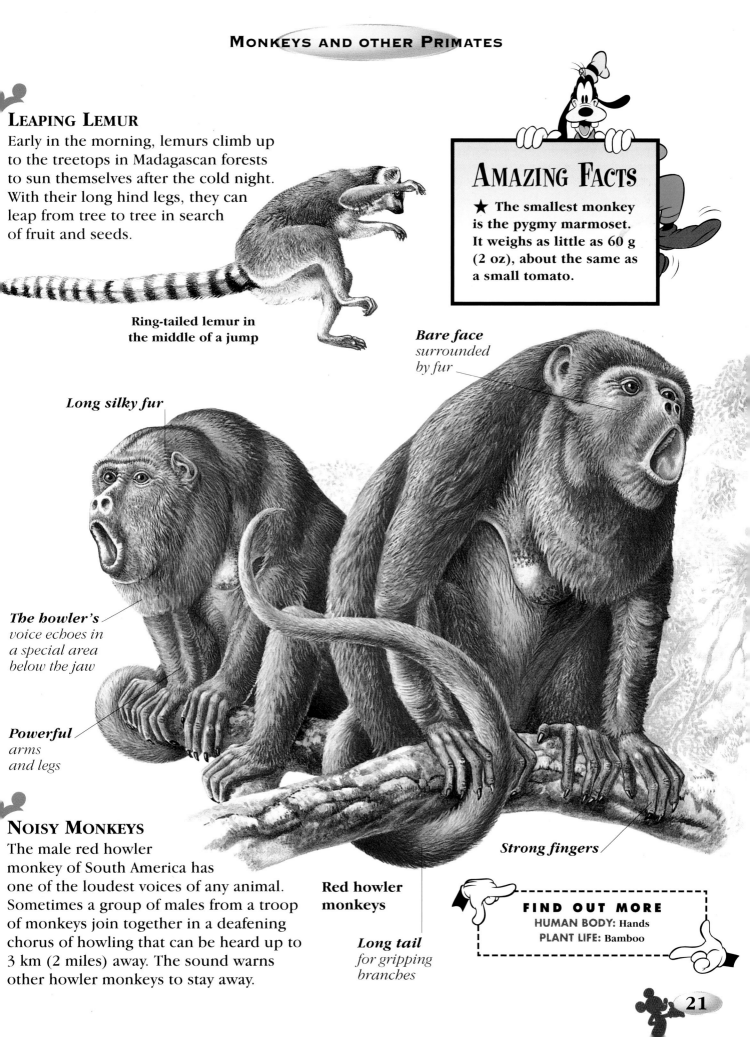

The Apes

Two male gorillas beating their chests and roaring at each other can seem very frightening, but this is a rare sight. These huge primates are usually gentle creatures. They spend most of their time sleeping, or feasting on plant leaves, stems, and fruit. Gorillas, chimpanzees, and orangutans are called the great apes. Gibbons are tree-living apes from southern Asia. They are smaller than the great apes and are called lesser apes.

Mild threat

Friendly

Fear

MAKING FACES
A chimpanzee shows its feelings with a variety of faces. It pushes out its lips to show friendship, and grins to expose its teeth and gums when it feels afraid or in danger.

THE LARGEST APES

The forests and mountains of West and Central Africa are home to gorillas – the largest living primates. An adult male gorilla usually weighs about 175 kg (385 lb). Gorillas live in troops of as many as 30 animals. Each troop includes a leading adult male, a few young males, and several females and young.

Adult males are called *silverbacks because of the silvery fur on their backs*

Adult *female*

Gorilla troop

Females feed young *on their milk until they are about two years old*

Apes can walk on all *fours, resting on the knuckles of their hands*

TREE-LIVING APES

Gibbons live in pairs of one male and one female. They spend their lives up in the trees. Using their extremely long arms, they move around by swinging from hand to hand through the branches.

Gibbons hanging from a vine

Females grooming

Chimpanzee searching for insects in a rotten tree stump

USING TOOLS

Chimpanzees have learned to use everyday objects as tools. They poke sticks into holes to see what is inside, taking grubs from rotten wood. They also "fish" termites and ants from their nests. The insects bite the stick with their pincers. The chimp then pulls out the stick and eats the clinging insects.

Strong teeth for chewing plants

Young male

AMAZING FACTS

★ The largest known gorilla weighed more than 310 kg (680 lb), more than five times the average human.

★ Chimpanzees can relieve sickness or pain by eating special leaves.

FIND OUT MORE
COMMUNICATIONS: Body language
HUMAN BODY: Feelings

The Arctic

One of the coldest and windiest places on Earth is the area around the North Pole. This is known as the Arctic. It includes the Arctic Ocean and the frozen land around it, called tundra. Tundra covers the northern parts of North America, Europe, and Asia.

Despite the cold, many mammals live in the Arctic, including reindeer, musk oxen, foxes, hares, bears, lemmings, and moose. Packs of wolves hunt caribou and young musk oxen. Small creatures, such as lemmings, burrow into the earth or snow to shelter from cold winds. The Arctic Ocean is also home to whales, as well as walruses and many kinds of seals.

Furry hood

Snowsuit

Arctic mammals have furry coats and a thick layer of fat to keep them warm. Humans need warm clothes instead

Warm shoes for walking through the snow

HUNTING ON THE ICE
Polar bears live on the edge of Arctic ice sheets. They feed mainly on seals, which they snatch from the water, often through a hole in the ice. The bear kills the seal with its huge paws.

Walruses feed on sea creatures, such as clams

Long, sharp tusks

Walrus

Polar bear

Gap in the ice where seals can come up for air

Powerful claws and large paws for killing prey

MUSK OXEN

Big herds of shaggy-haired musk oxen wander over tundra lands. If they are attacked by wolves or other hunters, they gather in a tight circle. Young oxen stand in the middle of the circle, where they are protected from danger.

Horns to the front, musk oxen form a defensive circle

CHANGING COATS

Some arctic animals change the color of their coats as the seasons change. In winter, they have white coats, so they are hard to see in the snow. In summer, when the snow has melted, their coats turn brown or gray to blend with the surrounding rocks and plants.

Arctic fox

Winter coat

Summer coat

Arctic hare

Winter coat

Summer coat

Waterproof fur helps to protect the polar bear from freezing water

A layer of thick fat, called blubber, beneath the skin keeps seals warm

Beluga whale

Beluga whales sometimes get trapped in breathing holes in the ice

Harp seal

FIND OUT MORE
ATLAS OF THE WORLD: Arctic
PLANET EARTH: North Pole

Wild Dogs

All pet dogs are related to wolves. Wolves and other wild dogs – such as coyotes and foxes – are all carnivores (meat-eaters). Their bodies are specially adapted for hunting other animals. They have excellent senses for finding prey, usually long legs to chase it, and sharp teeth for killing. Some wild dogs live and hunt in family groups called packs. Pack members share their food and defend each other against enemies.

1 **A pack of African hunting dogs begins chasing a group of wildebeest.**

Wolf pack leader *howling*

HOWLING AT THE MOON

Gray wolves live in packs of 5 to 20 animals, led by the strongest, or dominant, male. The pack guards its home area and howls loudly to warn off other packs. In some parts of the world, people believe that wolves howl at a new moon.

Each pack member obeys the dominant wolf

Gray wolves

2 The pack tries to separate one wildebeest – a young or sick animal – from the rest.

3 The dogs quickly surround the lone animal and move in for the kill.

CITY FOX

The red fox lives in areas ranging from forests to deserts in Asia, Europe and North America. It even comes into towns and cities, where it eats people's waste food.

Red fox searching a garbage sack for food

AMAZING FACTS

★ Dingoes are Australian wild dogs. Given the chance, they will hunt and kill sheep. To keep the dogs off the sheep-grazing lands of southeastern Australia, farmers built the world's longest fence. It stretches 4,887 km (3,307 miles).

Dingo

Bush dogs drinking at a stream

Fur may be *white, gray, brown, or black*

Tail is used *for balance and for signaling to other pack members*

Thick fur *keeps the wolf warm in cold weather*

Back feet have *four claws, and the front feet have five claws*

AMERICAN BUSH DOG

Bush dogs live in the forests and grasslands of Central and South America. They spend most of the day in an underground den. At night, they hunt in packs for mice and rats.

FIND OUT MORE
PLANET EARTH: Grasslands
SPACE: Moon

Bears

☞Bears are not as cuddly as they seem. When they are startled or feel threatened, they will attack with their strong teeth and claws. Bears are the largest flesh-eating land mammals, but they eat anything, including plants and insects. In fall, bears in cool climates eat as much as possible to build up stores of fat in their bodies. Then they hide away in a warm den, such as a cave or a tree hollow, where they sleep through the winter months, or hibernate.

AMAZING FACTS

★ Biggest of all the bears is the polar bear. It is 3 m (10 ft) long and weighs as much as 800 kg (1,750 lb).

★ The little sun bear weighs only 65 kg (145 lb).

GRIZZLY BEARS

Brown bears live in northern Europe, Asia, and North America, where they are called grizzlies. Plants are their main food, but they often eat insects and other small animals. They also catch and eat fish.

SPECTACLED BEAR

The spectacled bear lives in the Andes Mountains in South America. Light rings around the bear's eyes make it look as if it is wearing eyeglasses, or spectacles. A good climber, it finds its food in trees.

Spectacled
bear

Polar bears wrestling

FIGHTING PRACTICE

As young polar bears play, they develop the fighting skills they need as adults. Cubs stay with their mother for about 28 months, learning how to hunt in the icy Arctic.

Cubs live with their mother until they are four years old

Brown bear and cub catching fish

Sun bear

HONEY LOVER

The forests of Southeast Asia are the home of the sun bear. This bear uses its curved claws to hook fruit off branches and to tear off tree bark to find tasty insects. Its long tongue is ideal for licking honey out of bees' nests.

Heavy, strongly muscled body

Bear hooks salmon out of the water with its powerful arms

BAMBOO EATER

The giant panda has a huge appetite. It spends up to 15 hours each day eating as much as 20 kg (44 lb) of juicy bamboo leaves and stems.

Giant panda eating bamboo

Salmon

Strong claws

FIND OUT MORE
ANIMALS OF THE SEA: Salmon
INSECTS AND SPIDERS: Bees

Small Hunters

It is not necessary to be big to be a good hunter. Mongooses and civets are small hunting animals that feed mainly on meat. The agile mongoose can even attack and kill a deadly cobra. Another group of small hunters includes skunks, weasels, badgers, and otters. Some of these animals are very fierce, with sharp teeth for tearing their food apart. Many have long, slender bodies for chasing animals into their burrows.

AMAZING FACTS

★ A badger's sense of smell is up to 800 times better than ours.

★ Musk oil from the scent glands of civets may not sound sweet smelling, but it is an ingredient of many perfumes.

Stiff hairs on the mongoose's back protect it from the cobra's fangs

Newborn badgers live in a nursery chamber for eight weeks

Badgers in their set

LIVING UNDERGROUND
Groups of badgers live in underground burrows called sets, which they dig with their long claws. They come out at night to hunt for food.

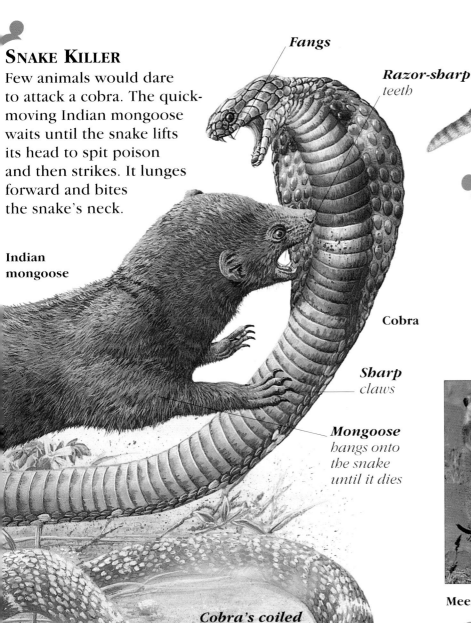

SNAKE KILLER

Few animals would dare to attack a cobra. The quick-moving Indian mongoose waits until the snake lifts its head to spit poison and then strikes. It lunges forward and bites the snake's neck.

Fangs

Razor-sharp *teeth*

Indian mongoose

Cobra

Sharp *claws*

Mongoose *hangs onto the snake until it dies*

Cobra's coiled *body ready to attack*

African palm civet

NIGHTTIME HUNTER

Civets are small mammals similar to cats. The palm civet is a skillful climber that spends most of its life in the trees. It comes out at night to hunt other small animals and to forage for fruit.

Meerkats watching for enemies

ON GUARD

The meerkat is a type of mongoose that lives in family groups in burrows. Some keep watch and bark warnings to the rest of the group when danger threatens, so they can take cover.

SMELLY SKUNK

When threatened, the skunk warns its enemy by waving its tail in the air and stamping. If the enemy does not go away, the skunk squirts jets of a bad-smelling oily liquid. This comes from special parts of the body, called scent glands, under its tail.

Tail raised, *ready to spray*

Striped skunk

FIND OUT MORE
PLANT LIFE: Life in the soil
REPTILES AND AMPHIBIANS: Cobra

31

Gobi Desert

Deserts are difficult places to live in. Although there is very little food, water, or shelter in a desert, some mammals manage to survive there. There are deserts in North and South America, Africa, Asia, and Australia.

Central Asia's Gobi Desert has baking hot summers, but chilly winters. Even in summer the temperature can drop by 20°C (36°F) at night. Many desert mammals survive the heat by avoiding it. They come out at night, dawn, or dusk, when it is cooler. Those that do come out in the day pant to cool down. Others have large ears that help get rid of body heat.

Hat

Light scarf

Long-sleeved top

Desert creatures have special ways of keeping cool in the day. People need to cover up for protection from the hot sun and blowing sand

Light *trousers*

DESERT JERBOA
The jerboa rarely drinks and can survive just on the water in its food. It comes out of its burrow at night to look for plants, seeds, and insects to eat. It may travel 12 km (7 miles) in one night as it searches for food.

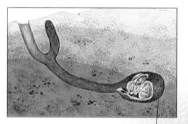

Long-eared jerboa

Jerboas dig a deep, cool burrow in which to shelter during the heat of the day

Nostrils and ears can be closed to keep out sand

Onager

The onager is a wild donkey that runs fast to escape enemies

Bactrian camel

DESERT DWELLER
The two-humped Bactrian camel can go without water for 10 months. When it does drink, it can take in 100 liters (26 gallons) in 10 minutes. The camel can survive for so long because it stores fat in its humps. The fat provides water and energy when food and drink are scarce.

Desert hedgehog

SPINY HEDGEHOG

The desert hedgehog feeds on birds, eggs, and scorpions. When threatened, it curls up into a ball. A hunter risks getting a mouthful of sharp spines if it tries to attack.

Humps
store fat

Goitered gazelle

Gazelles are the
onager's only real competitors for food in the Gobi Desert

Wide feet stop the
camel from sinking into the soft sand

MAMMALS OF THE STEPPES

The steppes are high, grassy plains that surround the Gobi Desert. The saiga antelope grazes on steppe grasses. Pallas's cat hunts at night. Its long, dense fur protects it from the icy winters.

Pallas's cat

Saiga antelope

FIND OUT MORE
INSECTS AND SPIDERS: Scorpions
PLANET EARTH: Deserts

33

Wild Cats

Cats are carnivores. They feed on the flesh of other animals – their prey. They have sharp teeth for killing their catches and powerful legs for running fast over short distances and jumping on prey. They have bendable backbones so that they can twist and turn easily when running. Cats rely mainly on their hearing and sight to find prey. Most hunt at night, when their large eyes enable them to see six times better than humans can.

A pride of lions in Kenya

LION FAMILIES
Lions live in family groups called prides. Each pride is made up of about a dozen animals, mainly females and their young, with one or more adult males.

POWERFUL TIGER
At dusk, the tiger – the biggest of all cats – hunts buffalo, deer, wild pigs, and other forest animals. Tigers live alone, roaring loudly to keep other tigers away. They mark their territory, or home range, with droppings, scent, and scratches on tree trunks.

Long whiskers *are sensitive to touch*

Sharp teeth *for eating prey*

Huge paws *can knock over prey with a single blow*

AMAZING FACTS
★ Lynxes have such good eyesight that they can spot a tiny mouse 75 m (250 ft) away.

★ Lions sleep for as long as 21 hours each day.

SMALL CATS
There are 30 species of small cats, such as the ocelot and the lynx. The ocelot of North and South America hunts mice, rats, and birds. The lynx of northern Europe and Asia hunts larger prey such as rabbits, hares, and small deer.

Eurasian lynx

Ocelot

Prey is dragged up *into a tree, away from other hunters that might steal the catch*

CLIMBING CAT
Leopards are often seen resting in the branches of trees. These excellent climbers sometimes leap straight out of a tree onto prey on the ground below. Leopards catch and eat any creatures from small insects to monkeys and pigs.

Leopard with prey

Spotted coat helps to *camouflage the leopard when it hunts among leaves and grasses*

PUMA FAMILY
Pumas live in North and South America. A female has two or more cubs, which start to hunt with her when they are six months old. About a year later, she drives them away to find food for themselves.

Puma and cubs

Stripes on a tiger's coat *help to break up the outline of its body so it is hard to see*

Indian tiger prowling through grass

FIND OUT MORE
HUMAN BODY: Eyes
REPTILES AND AMPHIBIANS: Camouflage

Sea Mammals

👉 Some mammals spend all or most of their lives in the sea. Their bodies are shaped for moving through water, and they have paddles or flippers for swimming instead of legs. They have to come to the surface of the water to breathe air. These sea mammals include whales, sea lions, seals, and dugongs. Under their skin, most sea mammals have a layer of fat, called blubber, that keeps them warm.

Dugong feeding

SHY SEA MAMMAL
The shy dugong feeds on sea plants. The sensitive bristles on its upper lip help it to find food on the sea floor. Dugongs live in small herds in the Indian and Pacific coastal waters.

A bag of skin on the nose puffs up to make the seal's roar louder

Fighting males attack each other's necks with open jaws

BATTLE OF THE GIANTS
The southern elephant seal is the largest of all seals. In the breeding season, a male seal gathers a group of females with whom he mates. If a rival male comes near, the two seals take up threatening positions and roar at each other.

Southern elephant seals on a subantarctic island

Sea lions sunning themselves

SPEEDY SEA LIONS
Sea lions may look lazy as they bask on land, but they are fast movers in water. California sea lions can swim as fast as 40 km/h (25 mph). All sea lions push themselves through the water with sweeps of their front flippers. Some seals swim by moving their strong back flippers.

MOLLUSK-EATER

A sea otter floats on its back when it is eating, using its chest as a table. It feeds on fish, sea urchins, clams, crabs, mussels, and snails. Sea otters do not have fatty blubber, but instead rely on their thick, waterproof fur to keep them warm.

Hard-shelled
food is smashed open on a rock

Rock

Sea otter

Trunklike snout
hangs over the upper lip

A male elephant seal
weighs up to 4,000 kg (8,800 lb) – as much as 60 people

Thick skin
has a sparse covering of hair

AMAZING FACTS

★ Before sea otters go to sleep in the water, they wrap themselves up in seaweed so they are not swept away.

★ Sailors long ago thought that dugongs were the imaginary beings called mermaids.

Hind flippers are
broad and fan-shaped

FIND OUT MORE
ANIMALS OF THE SEA: Sea urchins
PLANT LIFE: Sea plants

Thick layer of fat protects
the elephant seal from cold

37

Great Whales

Whales are the biggest of the sea mammals. There are two kinds – baleen and toothed. Baleen whales, such as blue whales and humpbacks, have bristly plates instead of teeth in their mouths. These are made of a material called baleen. To feed, the whales take in gulps of water. Tiny creatures are trapped on the baleen as the water drains out. Toothed whales, including dolphins, hunt for their food.

Grooves on the throat *allow the skin to stretch as the whale takes in water when feeding*

Fleshy knobs *or lumps on the snout*

Whales blow air and *water vapor out of a blowhole and breathe in again before diving*

Male humpback whale

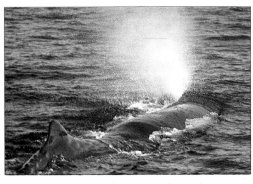

Sperm whale surfacing to breathe

DEEP DIVER
The sperm whale dives longer and deeper than any other mammal as it searches for squid to eat. The deepest recorded dive by a sperm whale is 2,000 m (6,560 ft), and the longest lasted nearly two hours.

SEA GIANT

The blue whale is the biggest animal on Earth today and probably the biggest ever to have lived – even bigger than the largest dinosaur. Female blue whales have been known to reach more than 33 m (108 ft) long. Blue whales live in all oceans.

300 baleen plates hang from the whale's upper jaw

The blue whale swims by moving its tail up and down

Human diver

SINGING WHALE

Male humpback whales are famous for their beautiful "songs." They sing for hours on end, pausing only briefly for breath. Each individual has his own song, made up of lots of different sounds. He uses these to attract females and frighten off other males.

Orcas surrounding a school of fish

Flippers help *the whale turn in the water*

GROUP HUNTERS

Orcas, or killer whales, are a type of dolphin. Like a pack of wolves, orcas hunt together, herding groups, or schools, of fish and then moving in for the kill. They also eat seals, squid, and even other whales. Sometimes they snatch seals from the seashore.

The humpback breaches, *or leaps out of the water, to send signals to other whales and may land on its back*

AMAZING FACTS

★ A baby blue whale is already 7 m (23 ft) long when it is born. It weighs 1,000 times more than a newborn human baby.

FIND OUT MORE
ANIMALS OF THE SEA: Squid
PLANET EARTH: Oceans

African Savanna

Vast, open plains, covered in grass and dotted with acacia trees, make up the African savanna. It is always hot, but most of the rain falls during a short period called the wet season. For the rest of the year, the land is very dry.

A rich variety of mammals lives in the savanna, including plant-eaters such as giraffes, elephants, zebras, antelopes, and gazelles. Leopards, lions, cheetahs, and hunting dogs hunt the plant-eaters. Scavengers such as hyenas wait to finish any leftovers.

SPEEDY RUNNERS

The savanna is home to some of the world's fastest mammals, such as cheetahs and gazelles. The cheetah cannot run fast for long, so gets as close as possible to its prey before starting the final, high-speed chase. If the cheetah does not succeed in catching its prey after about 400 m (1,320 ft), it gives up.

Acacia trees provide some shelter in the savanna

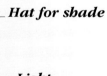

Male patas monkey keeps watch while the female feeds

Patas monkeys

Spotted coat helps the cheetah hide in the savanna grass

Hat for shade

Light clothing

Savanna animals try to stay out of the hot sun. Humans need light clothes and a brimmed hat when on safari

Strong boots for protection from insects and spiky grasses

Long tail helps the cheetah balance as it runs

Wildlife of the savanna

STRIPED COATS

Zebras are wild African horses. Their striking coats of black and white stripes may help zebras to recognize each other. Or they may make it more difficult for a hunting animal, such as a lion, to see them.

Migrating wildebeest

Herd of zebra at a waterhole

WANDERING WILDEBEEST

In the dry season, no rain falls, and water and grass are hard to find. Herds of up to 10,000 wildebeest migrate to find food. They walk long distances across the savanna in search of waterholes and grass.

When in danger, Thomson's gazelles spring up and down to confuse attackers

Thomson's gazelles

Cheetah

The cheetah is the fastest *land mammal and can run at 105 km/h (65 mph)*

FIND OUT MORE
ATLAS OF THE WORLD: Africa
PLANET EARTH: Savanna

41

Freshwater Mammals

Asian short-clawed otters

The fresh waters of rivers and lakes are home to a variety of plants, insects, fish, and small animals. These form a rich food supply for many different mammals, including otters, platypuses, and even some dolphins. (Most dolphins live in the sea, but a few kinds live in rivers.) Some large mammals, including hippopotamuses, like to be in water because it keeps them cool during the heat of the day.

FEELING FOR FOOD

The short-clawed otter of Southeast Asia has a delicate sense of touch. Using its paws, it feels around for food, such as fish or mollusks, in the soft mud of the river bed.

A hippo weighs up to 4,000 kg (8,800 lb)

WALLOWING HIPPOS

Hippos spend up to 16 hours each day wallowing in lakes and rivers. They swim well, but they usually prefer to walk along the river bottom. At sunset they leave the water to eat grass on land.

Birds perch nearby ready to pick scraps of food from between a hippo's teeth

Nostrils and eyes high on the head allow a hippo to see and breathe while in the water

Diving
platypus

AMAZING FACTS

★ The platypus is one of the few poisonous mammals. Males have a hollow claw on each back foot, which they use to jab into their enemies and inject poison.

DUCK-BILLED PLATYPUS

The platypus is an egg-laying mammal, with a beak like a duck. It lives in Australia, where it spends most of the day hiding in a burrow. At dusk and dawn, it comes out to hunt for food in water.

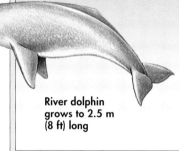

River dolphin grows to 2.5 m (8 ft) long

RIVER DOLPHINS

The long-beaked, almost blind Amazon River dolphin feeds on piranha fish, prawns, and crabs. Young animals are bluish-gray, but they become pinker as they get older.

Wide-open jaws warn
other males to stay away

Dam is made
of mud, branches, leaves, and grass

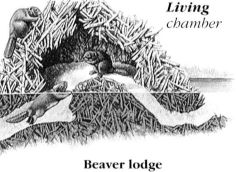

Living
chamber

Beaver lodge

Underwater
channels lead to living chamber

BEAVER BUILDERS

Beavers live in family groups in Europe and North America. With the help of their huge front teeth, they cut down trees and use the wood to build a dam. This creates a pond, where they build a nest, or lodge.

Teeth are up to
50 cm (20 in) long

Hippos in an African river

FIND OUT MORE
ATLAS OF THE WORLD: Amazon River
PLANET EARTH: Rivers

Hoofed Mammals

There are over 200 different kinds of hoofed mammals, which scientists call ungulates. They include the mighty rhinoceros as well as horses, cows, and pigs. All of them have toes that end in special hard coverings called hooves. Hooves are made of keratin – the same material as fingernails and claws. They are plant eaters, and most walk on the tips of their toes. Some hoofed mammals also have horns made of keratin on their heads.

Tusks are extra-large teeth

WILD BOAR

Fast-moving wild boars charge at enemies with their short, sharp tusks. Boars are the wild relatives of farmyard pigs. Like them, they use their long snouts to dig up roots, bulbs, nuts, and mushrooms to eat.

Przewalski's horse

WILD HORSE

Przewalski's horse was once common on the plains of Mongolia. But by 1969, experts could find no evidence of the horses in the wild. Animals bred in captivity have now been reintroduced to the wild.

Rhinos have good hearing but poor eyesight

INDIAN RHINO

Thick plates of skin make the mighty rhinoceros look as if it is wearing armor. Other horned mammals have horns on top of their heads, but rhinos have horns on their noses. Some rhinos have two horns, but the Indian rhino has just one.

Horn is made of thick, tightly packed keratin fibers

Thick skin falls into heavy folds

Indian rhino charging

Vicunas grazing in Peru

MOUNTAIN VICUNAS

Vicunas are the smallest members of the camel family, but they have no humps. They live high in the Andes Mountains in South America, protected from the cold winds by their thick, wooly coats.

AMAZING FACTS

★ The African white rhino weighs as much as 3,600 kg (8,000 lb). That is more than 50 average people.

Strong legs
to carry the
rhino's weight

Curved
horn

Water buffalo
wallowing in
water

LONG HORNS

Water buffalo live in herds of up to 50 animals in the marshes and wetlands of Southeast Asia. Their long, curved horns are a good defense against their main enemy – the tiger.

FIND OUT MORE
HUMAN BODY: Keratin
PLANT LIFE: Mushrooms

Heavy hooves
tip the three toes
on each foot

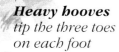

Grazing Mammals

Many hoofed mammals graze – they feed on grass and other ground plants. Others eat the leaves of shrubs and trees. Hoofed grazers, such as cattle, giraffes, and deer, eat in a special way. They swallow plants after chewing them briefly. The food is partly digested, or broken down, in the animal's stomach and then brought back into the mouth for a more thorough chew. This is called chewing the cud.

The giraffe's tongue is up to 45 cm (18 in) long

Giraffes at a waterhole

TALLEST MAMMALS
Giraffes are the tallest living mammals – their heads are about 5.3 m (17 ft) above ground. They feed on treetop leaves that other animals on the African savanna cannot reach.

Stumpy horns *are made of bone, covered by skin*

Male ibex perching on a rocky ledge

SURE-FOOTED IBEX
These goat-antelopes can move rapidly over rocky mountain slopes. They leap from rock to rock with ease. Male ibexes have large, backward-curving horns that may grow to more than 75 cm (29 in) long.

SPEEDY ANTELOPE

The fast-running, long-legged impala is a type of antelope. Impalas live in herds of 15 to 25 females and young, led by a single adult male. When an attacker threatens, the impalas flee in all directions, leaping away at high speed.

Impala

The front legs are *spread wide apart when the giraffe bends to drink*

Long tail *is used to flick away flies*

Skin pattern helps to *camouflage the giraffe*

Long neck has *seven bones, as in other mammals, but each bone is very long*

AMAZING FACTS

★ **Even newborn giraffes are 2 m (7 ft) tall.**

★ **No two giraffes have exactly the same pattern on their skin.**

FIGHTING SAMBAR

Male sambar deer, or stags, have big branching horns called antlers on their heads. They use their antlers to impress females and to fight other males for the right to mate with females.

Male sambar deer lock antlers in a fight

FIND OUT MORE
INSECTS AND SPIDERS: Flies
REPTILES AND AMPHIBIANS: Camouflage

Elephants

An elephant's trunk is like an all-purpose tool. It is strong enough to lift heavy tree trunks and yet so sensitive that it can pick ripe fruit without damaging it. The trunk is also used for smelling, washing, breathing, feeling, and making loud trumpeting sounds. Tusks, too, have many uses, including digging for roots and water, and fighting off enemies. There are two kinds of elephant – African and Asian.

ASIAN ELEPHANT

The Asian elephant weighs up to 5,400 kg (11,900 lb) and stands 3.4 m (11 ft) tall at the shoulder. At the end of its trunk is a projection like a finger that helps the elephant hold things.

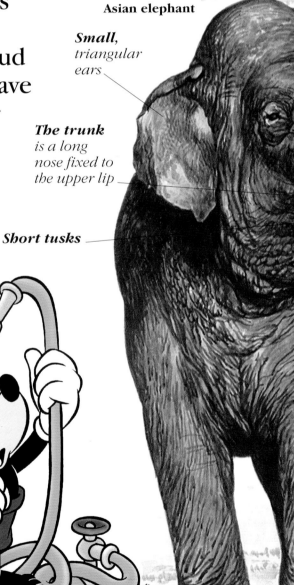

Asian elephant

Small, triangular ears

The trunk is a long nose fixed to the upper lip

Short tusks

BATHTIME

Elephants live in hot countries, so they need to stay cool. They often give themselves a refreshing shower by sucking up water with their trunks and spraying it over their bodies.

An African elephant bathing

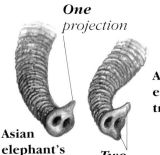

One projection

Asian elephant's trunk

African elephant's trunk

Two projections

AFRICAN ELEPHANT

African elephants can grow to more than 4 m (13 ft) tall at the shoulder and weigh about 6,000 kg (13,200 lb). Their trunks have two fingerlike projections on the end.

African elephant

AMAZING FACTS

★ Elephants eat at least 150 kg (330 lb) of plant food each day. That is about as much as 1,000 apples or pears.

Larger, more rounded ears than the Asian elephant

WORKING ELEPHANTS

An elephant's trunk contains as many as 100,000 muscles, making it very strong. For thousands of years, people have trained elephants to lift, push, and drag heavy objects.

Elephant lifting a heavy log with its powerful trunk

Skin is up to 2.5 cm (1 in) thick

Long tusks

Tusks are giant teeth

Young African elephants

BIG BABY

A newborn elephant is a big baby, weighing up to twice as much as the average adult human. The baby needs to feel close to its mother, so it often holds onto her tail with its trunk as she walks.

FIND OUT MORE
PAINTING AND SCULPTURE: Hindu art
STORY OF THE PAST: Elephants in battle

49

The Himalayas

The world's highest peaks are found in the Himalayas. This mountain range stretches about 2,400 km (1,500 miles) across parts of India, Nepal, and Tibet.

Many mammals, including bears, deer, and wolves live on the lower slopes of the mountains. Only a few, such as yaks, survive higher up. Some small mammals, such as marmots, hibernate, or sleep, through the coldest months of the year. While they sleep, their heartbeat and breathing slow so they use as little energy as possible.

MOUNTAIN BURROWERS

Bobak marmots live in underground burrows and come out in the early morning to feed. One marmot keeps watch and warns the others of any danger with a shrill alarm signal.

Bobak marmot

SACRED LANGUR

The graceful Hanuman langur of the Himalayan foothills is sacred to people of the Hindu religion. A kind of monkey, it represents the Hindu monkey god Hanuman. It eats leaves, fruit, and flowers.

Hanuman langurs live together in groups

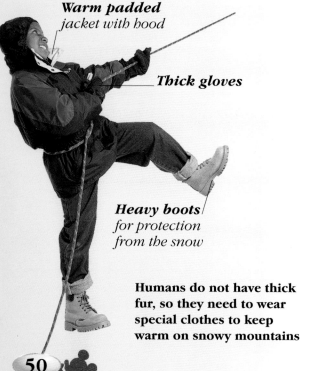

Warm padded jacket with hood

Thick gloves

Heavy boots for protection from the snow

Humans do not have thick fur, so they need to wear special clothes to keep warm on snowy mountains

Snow leopard chasing prey

HIMALAYAN CAT

The thick-furred snow leopard hunts wild sheep and goats. In summer, the snow leopard roams up to heights of 5,500 m (18,000 ft). In winter, it follows its prey down to the lower, forested mountain slopes.

BLENDING IN

Blue sheep do not run from danger – they just stand still so they are hard to see. Their slate-gray coats are a bluish color, which helps them blend in well with the rocky Himalayan landscape. Blue sheep eat grass and plantlike lichens.

Blue sheep in the Himalayas

Mountain animals

Mountain peaks are often stormy and windy

Shaggy coat

Yak

Curved horns

The takin *has strong legs to help it climb*

Takin

The markhor *is a wild goat with corkscrew-shaped horns*

Markhor

MOUNTAIN DWELLER

The yak is one of the world's highest-living animals. With its thick, ragged hair and a densely matted underfur, the yak is well protected against freezing temperatures.

Mountain flowers

FIND OUT MORE
ATLAS OF THE WORLD: **Himalayas**
PLANT LIFE: **Lichens**

Rodents and Rabbits

Mice and rats are members of an amazingly successful group of mammals called rodents. They include squirrels, beavers, hamsters, and capybaras. All have two large teeth at the front of each jaw that keep growing all through the rodent's life. The teeth do not grow too long because they are worn down as the rodent chews, or gnaws, tough food such as seeds and grass. Long-eared rabbits and hares are also gnawing animals.

SPEEDY RABBITS

Rabbits are fast-running mammals with long back legs. Large groups of rabbits live together in burrows they dig in the ground. At night they come out to find food.

Common rabbit

RATS AND PEOPLE

Most rats live in forests and have little contact with human beings. Brown and black rats, however, live in cities and towns all over the world. They come out at night to eat any food they can find.

Indian giant squirrel

GIANT SQUIRRELS

Unlike most other rodents, which are active at night, squirrels come out during the day. Many have bushy tails and live in trees. The giant squirrel of Southeast Asia eats nuts, bark, and insects, and often steals fruit from farms.

Scaly tail

Small, neat ears

Front paws are used to hold food

Grain is a favorite food of rats and mice

Capybara

Mouse

RODENT GIANT
The largest of all rodents is the capybara. It is 1.4 m (4½ ft) long and weighs 66 kg (145 lb) – a giant compared to a mouse. The capybara lives near water in forests and grasslands in Central and South America.

CRESTED PORCUPINE
If a porcupine is threatened by another animal, it raises the sharp spines on its back as a defense. If the attacker does not go away, the porcupine runs backward into its enemy so the spines stick into its body.

Porcupine with raised spines

Long, coarse fur protects the rat from cold and damp

Long, sensitive whiskers

Back teeth are used to grind up food

Brown rats attacking a sack of grain

FIND OUT MORE
PLANT LIFE: Fruit, Grains

Mammals at Risk

Many mammals are now rare. Some have become extinct, or died out completely, because they were hunted in huge numbers. Today, others are in danger as industry and farming destroys the places in which they live. Many kinds of rare mammals are now protected by laws. Some live free from human disturbance in special areas called wildlife reserves.

Baby orangutans in the Sandakan sanctuary

HELPING THE ORANGUTANS
Numbers of wild orangutans are falling. The orangutan sanctuary at Sandakan in Sabah, Malaysia, aims to teach local people and tourists about how to protect these rare jungle mammals.

Orca surfacing near a tour boat

WHALE WATCHING
In New Zealand and other areas where whales can be seen, boats take people to view them at close hand. These trips help people to understand more about whales and to care about their well-being.

Tourists on safari watching giraffes

ON SAFARI

Travelers once paid to hunt and kill lions and other large animals. Today, people prefer to take home pictures instead of animal skins. They take photos from their vehicle, which masks the smell of the humans so the animals are not frightened or disturbed.

AMAZING FACTS

★ An area of rain forest the size of 50 soccer fields is destroyed by human activity every minute. At least half the world's plant and animal species live in rain forests, and many are now at risk of extinction.

This rhino's horn has been painlessly removed to protect it from poachers

HORNLESS RHINOCEROS

Rhinos are now very rare. Many have been killed for their horns, which are used to make jewelry and medicines. Wildlife rangers often saw off the horns to save the rhinos from poachers.

BREEDING IN CAPTIVITY

Some rare animals are bred in zoos. The Arabian oryx is the world's rarest antelope. Some have been born in captivity and taken back to the wild. A herd of about 00 oryx now roams the rabian desert once again.

Arabian oryx

FIND OUT MORE
ATLAS OF THE WORLD: Malaysia
REPTILES AND AMPHIBIANS: Conservation

Glossary of Key Words

Antler: A large, branching horn.

Ape: A large primate.

Backbone: A series of small bones, called vertebrae, that run the length of an animal's body; also called the spine.

Baleen: The bristly fringes inside a whale's mouth to trap food.

Blubber: The thick layer of fat under some animals' skins that protects them from cold.

Breach: The leap of a whale out of the water.

Breeding season: The time of year when mammals mate.

Burrow: An underground hole where an animal makes its nest.

Camouflage: The special colors and patterns that help an animal blend in with its surroundings.

Carnivore: An animal that mainly eats the flesh of other animals.

Chewing the cud: When an animal, such as a cow, chews and swallows plants, partly digests them, and then brings them back up to chew again.

Climate: The type of weather that is usual for a particular area.

Den: The home of an animal, such as a bear.

Extinction: The process by which all individuals of a species, or particular type, die out.

Flipper: A paddle-shaped limb used to swim with.

Graze: To eat grass and other growing plants.

Grooming: When an animal cleans or combs through fur to remove dirt.

Herbivore: An animal that feeds only on plants.

Herd: A large number of the same kind of animals that live together.

Hibernate: To fall into a deep, sleeplike state to survive cold winter months.

Hoof: A hornlike covering at the end of some mammals' feet.

Horn: A keratin-covered growth on an animal's head.

Keratin: The material that makes up fingernails, toenails, claws, horns, hooves, and scales.

Mammal: An animal that gives birth to live young and does not lay eggs. Mammals feed their babies on milk from their bodies.

Mammary gland: The part of a female mammal's body that produces milk to feed her babies.

Marsupial: A mammal that gives birth to its babies before they are fully developed. The babies continue growing in a pouch on the outside of the mother's body.

Mating: When a male and female get together to produce young.

Pack: A group of animals, such as dogs, that survives by living and hunting together.

Poacher: A person who illegally kills animals.

Predator: An animal that hunts other animals for food.

Prey: An animal that is hunted by other animals for food.

Pride: A family group of lions.

Primate: A mammal that has a large brain and hands that can grasp things. Apes, monkeys, and humans are primates.

Quill: One of many long, sharp, hollow spines that cover an animal such as a porcupine.

Rodent: A small mammal with large teeth at the front of each jaw for gnawing.

Safari: A trip into the wild to observe wild animals close up.

Sanctuary: A place of safety that people have established where animals can live undisturbed and free from poachers.

Scavenger: An animal, such as a hyena, that eats dead meat left by other animals.

Scent gland: The part of an animal's body that produces strong-smelling chemicals.

Skeleton: The bony frame that supports and protects a body.

Snout: The long nose of an animal such as an anteater.

Species: A particular type of animal whose individuals are very similar and can breed together.

Sweat gland: The part of an animal's body that releases a watery fluid onto the skin to help keep the animal cool.

Territory: The special area where an animal lives and finds its food, and that it often defends.

Troop: A family group of animals such as monkeys.

Trunk: A flexible, muscular nose joined to an elephant's upper lip.

Tusk: A long, pointed tooth.

Ungulate: A mammal with hooves, such as a horse.

Vertebrae: The interlocking bones that make up an animal's spine, or backbone.

Warm blooded: When an animal is able to keep a constant body temperature.

Index

(*see* **Famous Places** for a full index to your complete set of books)

57